Math in the Kitchen
Fractions

Ian F. Mahaney

PowerKiDS press.

New York

Published in 2013 by The Rosen Publishing Group, Inc.
29 East 21st Street, New York, NY 10010

First Edition

Editor: Joanne Randolph
Book Design: Greg Tucker

Photo Credits: Cover AISPIX by Image Source/Shutterstock.com; p. 5 Rob Marmion/Shutterstock.com; p. 6 Tom Grill/The Image Bank/Getty Images; p. 7 Smit/Shutterstock.com; p. 8 AsiaSelects/Getty Images; p. 9 Scholastic Studio 10/Photolibrary/Getty Images; p. 10 Philip and Karen Smith/Iconica/Getty Images; p. 11 erashov/Shutterstock.com; p. 12 Eak/Shutterstock.com; p. 13 Anatoliy Samara/Shutterstock.com; pp. 14–15 Henglein & Streets/Cultura/Getty Images; pp. 16–17 Monkey Business Images/Shutterstock.com; p. 19 Comstock Images/Thinkstock; pp. 20–21 Adie Bush/Cultura/Getty Images.

Library of Congress Cataloging-in-Publication Data

Mahaney, Ian F.
 Math in the kitchen : fractions / by Ian F. Mahaney. — 1st ed.
    p. cm. — (Core math skills)
 Includes index.
 ISBN 978-1-4488-9656-1 (library binding) — ISBN 978-1-4488-9770-4 (pbk.) —
 ISBN 978-1-4488-9771-1 (6-pack)
 1. Fractions—Juvenile literature. I. Title.
 QA117.M235 2013
 513.2′6—dc23
                                    2012025150

Manufactured in the United States of America

CPSIA Compliance Information: Batch #W13PK4: For Further Information contact Rosen Publishing, New York, New York at 1-800-237-9932

Contents

Math Is Everywhere

Math is part of everything we do. Even when you are in the kitchen, you can practice math! You measure, count, and use time in the kitchen. When a **recipe** calls for $\frac{1}{2}$ cup flour, you need to understand fractions. We will take a closer look at fractions in the kitchen.

Fractions help us understand parts of a **whole number**. Often, people cut sandwiches in two pieces. Together, the two pieces make up the whole sandwich. However, we need fractions to talk about how one of the pieces relates to the whole. This fraction is $\frac{1}{2}$.

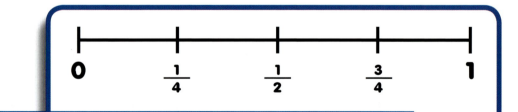

Looking at fractions on a number line may help you understand how fractions relate to whole numbers. It can help you compare fractions of different sizes, too. Here you can see that $\frac{1}{4}$ is smaller than $\frac{3}{4}$ because it comes first on the number line.

When we measure ingredients for a recipe, we are using fractions in the kitchen.

An orange is cut into four pieces. What fraction shows one piece of the orange?

(See answers on p. 22)

Figure It Out

Pizza Fractions

What is more fun than pizza for dinner? Many pizzas are cut into eight equal **slices**. One slice is $\frac{1}{8}$ of a pizza. This fraction shows that one slice is part of a whole pizza. Similarly, two slices can be **expressed** as $\frac{2}{8}$ of a pizza. A **diagram** can help you understand parts of a pizza and other fractions:

$\frac{1}{8}$ of a pizza $\frac{2}{8}$ of a pizza

Fractions have two parts. The top number is the numerator. The bottom number is the denominator. In a pizza, the denominator is the total number of slices.

Can you figure out what fraction of this pizza is missing? How about what is left? Start by counting the slices, and do not forget the missing slice. You will see that $\frac{1}{8}$ is gone, and $\frac{7}{8}$ is left.

If you eat two slices of a pizza that has six slices, how much of the pizza did you eat?

(See answers on p. 22)

Figure It Out

Breakfast by the Numbers

You can start your day with fractions at breakfast. Some boxes of cereal have 11 **servings**. That means that when you eat one serving of cereal, you have eaten $\frac{1}{11}$ of the cereal in the box.

If you pour one serving, or 8 ounces, of milk on your cereal from 1 quart of milk, which is 32 ounces, you have poured $\frac{8}{32}$ of the milk. This can be simplified by dividing both numbers by 8 to give you $\frac{1}{4}$.

When a family of five eats one serving each, we can figure out what portion of the box they have eaten by adding the fractions: $\frac{1}{11} + \frac{1}{11} + \frac{1}{11} + \frac{1}{11} + \frac{1}{11} = \frac{5}{11}$. When denominators are the same, you can add fractions by adding the numerators and placing the sum over the denominator.

Figure It Out

Most eggs are sold by the dozen, so there are 12 in a carton. If you open a new carton and fry two eggs, then your brother boils one egg, what fraction of the eggs have you cooked together?

(See answers on p. 22)

Time to Go!

There are 60 minutes in an hour. Pretend you have 45 minutes to eat breakfast and walk to school. That is $\frac{45}{60}$ of an hour.

It takes you 15 minutes to eat. To **determine** the time you have to walk to school, you can subtract the numerators if the denominators are the same. The remaining time you have to walk to school is $\frac{45}{60} - \frac{15}{60} = \frac{30}{60}$ of an hour. That is 30 minutes. You can simplify $\frac{30}{60}$ by dividing the numerator and denominator by 30: $30 \div 30 = 1$ and $60 \div 30 = 2$. Your new fraction is $\frac{1}{2}$, or half an hour.

Fifteen minutes is $\frac{15}{60}$ of an hour. You can simplify $\frac{15}{60}$ by dividing the numerator and denominator by 15: $15 \div 15 = 1$ and $60 \div 15 = 4$. Your new fraction is $\frac{1}{4}$. Fifteen minutes is one-quarter of an hour!

Figure It Out

If dinner is in an hour and you have 50 minutes of homework to do, how much free time will you have after you finish your homework and before dinner? Can you express it in a fraction?

(See answers on p. 22)

Lunch Fractions

You can show your fraction **skills** at lunch, too. Do you remember the sandwich cut in half in chapter 1? That sandwich has two parts. What would you do if you needed four parts to share your sandwich with three friends? You can make four pieces by cutting the halves in half again. Each piece is $\frac{1}{4}$ of the sandwich.

If each of these people has $\frac{1}{2}$ sandwich, how many whole sandwiches were there? You can figure this out by counting how many halves there are. There are six, which we can write as $\frac{6}{2}$. If you divide the top and bottom by 2, $6 \div 2 = 3$ and $2 \div 2 = 1$, you get $\frac{3}{1}$, or three sandwiches.

Whole numbers like 2 and 3 can be made into fractions. Place a 1 in the denominator of any whole number to make the fractions $\frac{2}{1}$ and $\frac{3}{1}$. Making whole numbers into fractions will help you multiply fractions in the next chapter.

Figure It Out

How many pieces of sandwich will there be if you cut all four pieces in half again? What is the fraction that shows how much of the sandwich one of those pieces is?

(See answers on p. 22)

Baking Dessert

To multiply fractions, multiply the numerators and put the product in the numerator of the answer. Then multiply the denominators and put the product in the denominator of the answer. Here is an example in the kitchen.

Ed finds a recipe for 8 cookies:

1 cup flour

$\frac{1}{2}$ cup sugar

$\frac{1}{2}$ teaspoon baking soda

$\frac{1}{2}$ cup butter

1 egg

1 cup chocolate chips

He decides to **double** the recipe and bake 16 cookies. Doubling means he will multiply all the ingredients by two. When multiplying fractions by 2, 2 can be expressed as the fraction $\frac{2}{1}$. For example, he will need:

2 x 1 = 2 cups flour

$2 \times \frac{1}{2} = \frac{2}{1} \times \frac{1}{2} = \frac{2 \times 1}{1 \times 2} = \frac{2}{2}$ cup sugar. Finishing that with division results in 1 cup sugar.

If you have ever baked before, then you know that measuring cups are marked by fractions. Now you know what to do with those fractions, too!

Can you finish the recipe? You will need to double $\frac{1}{2}$ teaspoon baking soda, $\frac{1}{2}$ cup butter, 1 egg, and 1 cup chocolate chips.

(See answers on p. 22)

Figure It Out

Snack Math

It is a good thing you have learned about fractions because it is snack time. Today's snack is grapes. There are 60 grapes in the bunch that will be split among four kids. You could hand each kid one grape at a time until the grapes run out, or you can use fractions.

The grapes need to be split four ways so each kid will have $\frac{1}{4}$ of 60 grapes. You can find the answer by multiplying the fraction by the whole number: $\frac{1}{4}$ x 60. Remember that multiplying by $\frac{1}{4}$ is the same as dividing by 4: $\frac{60}{4} = 15$. Each kid will get 15 grapes.

If you have 50 carrot sticks and you eat 20, what fraction of the carrot sticks have you eaten? You can write it this way: $\frac{20}{50} = \frac{20 \div 10}{50 \div 10} = \frac{2}{5}$. You have eaten two-fifths of the carrots!

There are 64 ounces of juice in a bottle to be split among eight people. How many ounces of juice does each person get?

(See answers on p. 22)

Figure It Out

17

Dinner Division

Say there are three containers of potato salad in your refrigerator. Each one weighs 2 pounds and your family eats one container at dinner. You say, "We ate $\frac{1}{3}$ of the potato salad." Your sister says, "No, we ate $\frac{2}{6}$ of the potato salad." You are both right.

Using lines to stand for the numbers on the number line can make it easier to see how the numbers in red relate to each other.

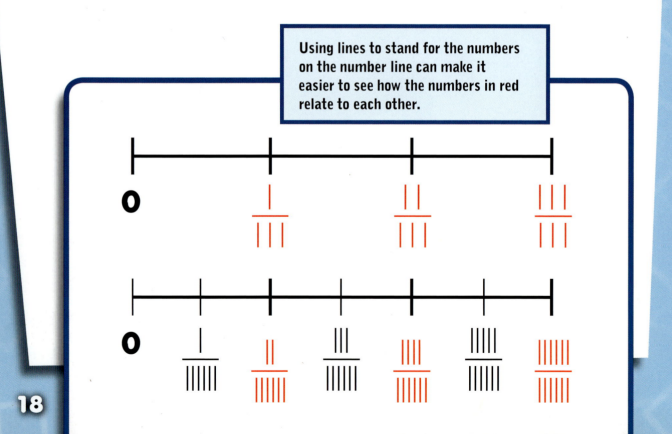

There are two ways to express the amount of potato salad you ate. One is that you have eaten one of three containers of potato salad. The other is that you ate 2 of 6 pounds of potato salad. These fractions are **equivalent**, and the number line can help you compare them.

Let's say you make **15** servings of lasagna for dinner. If you invite **10** guests, and everyone has one serving, what fraction of the lasagna did you eat? You can figure out the fraction this way: $\frac{10}{15} = \frac{10 \div 5}{15 \div 5} = \frac{2}{3}$.

What fractions are equivalent to $\frac{1}{2}$? You can multiply the numerator and denominator by the same number to figure this out.

(See answers on p. 22)

Figure It Out

Fractions in the Kitchen

You have learned how to understand fractions as part of a whole. You have also added fractions and subtracted fractions. You have even multiplied fractions and divided amounts of food. Great job!

There are many more fractions you can find in the kitchen. If there are four bananas on your counter, which weigh 1 pound total, each banana weighs $\frac{1}{4}$ pound. There are spices to measure and coffee to make. How many more fractions can you think of in the kitchen?

Next time you are in the kitchen, pay attention and see when you are using fractions. Fractions in the kitchen can be fun and tasty!

If a recipe calls for $\frac{1}{4}$ teaspoon vanilla, how much vanilla will you need if you triple the recipe?

(See answers on p. 22)

Figure It Out

Figure It Out: The Answers

Page 5: **The piece is one of four pieces of the orange. This fraction is $\frac{1}{4}$.**

Page 7: **You have eaten two of six slices, which is $\frac{2}{6}$ of the pizza.**

Page 9: **You have cooked $\frac{2}{12}$ of the eggs. Your brother has cooked $\frac{1}{12}$. Together, you have cooked $\frac{2}{12} + \frac{1}{12} = \frac{3}{12}$ of the eggs.**

Page 11: **An hour is $\frac{60}{60}$ of an hour. You do homework for $\frac{50}{60}$ of an hour. Your free time before dinner is the difference, $\frac{60}{60} - \frac{50}{60} = \frac{10}{60}$ of an hour, or 10 minutes.**

Page 13: **Cutting four pieces of sandwich in half makes eight pieces. Each of those is $\frac{1}{8}$ of the sandwich.**

Page 15: **Doubling the baking soda results in $\frac{2}{1}$ x $\frac{1}{2}$ = 2 x $\frac{1}{1}$ x 2 = $\frac{2}{2}$ teaspoon. When you divide, this gets you 1 teaspoon baking soda. Doubling the butter requires $\frac{2}{1}$ x $\frac{1}{2}$ = $\frac{2 \times 1}{1 \times 2}$ = $\frac{2}{2}$ cup. Dividing, this gets you 1 cup butter. Doubling the egg is 2 x 1 = 2 eggs. Doubling the chocolate chips is 2 x 1 = 2 cups chocolate chips.**

Page 17: **Each person will get $\frac{1}{8}$ of the juice. Dividing 64 by 8 will tell us how much juice each person gets: $\frac{64}{8}$ = 8.**

Page 19: **There are too many to list. Here are a few: $\frac{2}{4}$, $\frac{4}{8}$, and $\frac{5}{10}$ are equivalent to $\frac{1}{2}$.**

Page 21: **Tripling means multiplying by 3. To multiply $\frac{1}{4}$ teaspoon by 3, 3 needs to be a fraction. To triple the recipe requires $\frac{3}{1}$ x $\frac{1}{4}$ = $\frac{3 \times 1}{1 \times 4}$ = $\frac{3}{4}$ teaspoon vanilla.**

Glossary

determine (dih-TER-min) To figure out and decide.

diagram (DY-uh-gram) A picture of something.

double (DUH-bul) To make twice the amount.

equivalent (ih-KWIV-lent) Equal.

expressed (ik-SPRESD) Said mathematically.

recipe (REH-suh-pee) A set of directions for cooking.

servings (SER-vingz) Portions of food.

slices (SLYS-ez) Thin, flat pieces cut from something larger, such as a pizza.

skills (SKILZ) Abilities or things that help one do a job well.

whole number (HOHL NUM-ber) One of the counting numbers 1, 2, 3, and so on.

Index

Websites

Due to the changing nature of Internet links, PowerKids Press has developed an online list of websites related to the subject of this book. This site is updated regularly. Please use this link to access the list: www.powerkidslinks.com/cms/kitch/